Classic
Haiku

Classic Haiku

The Greatest Japanese Poetry
from Bashō, Buson, Issa, Shiki
and their Followers

Edited and introduced by
Tom Lowenstein

Photographs by
John Cleare

DUNCAN BAIRD PUBLISHERS
LONDON

Classic Haiku
Edited and introduced by Tom Lowenstein
Photographs by John Cleare

Distributed in the USA and Canada by
Sterling Publishing Co., Inc.
387 Park Avenue South,
New York, NY 10016-8810

This edition first published in the
UK and USA in 2007 by
Duncan Baird Publishers Ltd
Sixth Floor, Castle House
75–76 Wells Street, London W1T 3QH

Front cover image: *View of Trees Along
the Riverbank* from *Eight Views of the Xiao
and Xiang Rivers* by Shokei (Burnstein
Collection/Corbis)

The right of Tom Lowenstein to be identified
as the Author of this text has been asserted
in accordance with the Copyright, Designs and
Patents Act of 1988.

Editors: Kirty Topiwala and Susannah Marriott
Managing Designer: Clare Thorpe
Picture Editor: Julia Brown
Designer: Jerry Goldie

Library of Congress Cataloging-in-Publication
Data Available

ISBN: 978-1-84483-486-0

10 9 8 7 6 5 4 3 2

Typeset in Present and Skia
Printed in China
Color reproduction by Colourscan, Singapore

For information about custom editions, special
sales, premium and corporate purchases, please
contact Sterling Special Sales Department at
800-805-5489 or specialsales@sterlingpub.com.

Notes:
Abbreviations used throughout this book:
CE Common Era (the equivalent of AD)
BCE Before the Common Era (the equivalent
of BC)
b. born, **d.** died

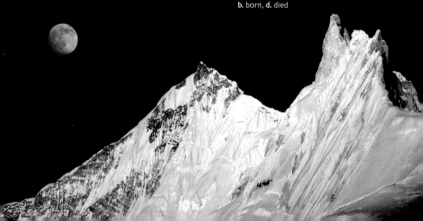

Contents

Introduction

Haiku are short, brilliantly vivid poems containing visually complete descriptions of moments in a poet's experience. In the space of their original 17 Japanese syllables, haiku express worlds of profound emotion and philosophical insight. Simple on the surface, yet fascinatingly complex on close study, haiku have universal appeal, and the number of languages into which they have been translated testify to this. Nonetheless, haiku retain a distinctly Japanese cultural flavour, and so to be able to interpret and enjoy the form, it is helpful to explore something of their history and background.

The classical background

In the many centuries before the development of haiku in the 17th century, Japanese poetry had a varied history. And while every successful haiku is fresh and unique, much of what we value so highly in the work of poets represented in this anthology is anticipated in the poetry that preceded them — often by a thousand years. This is not to deny the originality of later haiku poets. Rather, it helps us to identify the ways in which the poets worked within and modified the literary traditions they inherited.

Much, though not all, early Japanese poetry was written by the nobility, and despite the strict conventions of behaviour imposed on courtiers of the 8th to the 11th centuries, much of their poetry still radiates inspiration and sparkle today. A love of natural beauty infuses much early Japanese

writing, inspired partly by the Shinto religion with its emphasis on the spiritual presences inhabiting landscapes. This poem by Prince Shiki (668–716ᴄᴇ) is an exclamation of joy:

Bracken sprouts

above the stream that

rushes over rocks.

Spring is here!   PRINCE SHIKI

Nature images, such as cherry blossom, in early Japanese poetry became one of the most characteristic features of the canon. In other poems, such as this by the 8th-century poet Takechi no Kurohito, a note of melancholy suffuses the poet's vivid perception, and the snapshot of natural beauty is modulated by the suggestion of human activity, a technique often used by haiku poets many centuries later:

Travelling and lonely, I see beneath a hill

a boat painted with red clay rowing to the other side.

                                                 KUROHITO

From earliest times, a tradition of personal expression suffuses Japanese poetry. Here is a famously beautiful and proud 9th-century woman poet, Ono no Komachi, comparing her own fading beauty with the transience of nature:

No one minded that

the flowers' beauty faded.

And I saw myself in the world grow old

As the rain went on falling.   KOMACHI

Writers of the medieval period in Japan, from roughly the 8th to the 13th centuries, produced an enormous literature of love poetry. Most of the poems in Lady Murasaki's prose classic *The Tale of Genji* were short verses of longing, sadness or reminiscence exchanged between friends or lovers. The following verses traded between Prince Genji and the Japanese Empress at the death-bed of Genji's wife are characteristic. His poem comes first; hers answers:

In the haste we make to leave this world of dew,

May there be no time between the first and last.

GENJI

A world of dew before the autumn winds.

Not only theirs, these fragile leaves of grass.

EMPRESS

Murasaki continues: "Gazing at the two of them each somehow more beautiful than the other, Genji wished that he might have them a thousand years just as they were; but, of course, time runs against these wishes. That is the great sad truth." This sad truth about transience is an expression of the Buddhist doctrine that all beings are impermanent. The inherent sadness in life's transient incompleteness is a theme that would preoccupy the great haiku poets.

A knowledge of the classical poetic tradition represented in the 8th-century anthology *Man'yoshu* and the 10th-century *Kokinshu* (the first anthology to be assembled by court order so as to consolidate a national poetry in contradistinction to the Chinese tradition) was indispensable to later poets writing haiku. It is worth noting how poems from the past underlay some of the most striking compositions of later writers. For example, the great 8th-century poet Kakinamoto no Hitomaro wrote a lament on the death of his wife exploring the recurring theme of impermanence. Hitomaro's lines are echoed by the 18th-century poet Buson (incidentally writing long before his wife died!):

I come home to our room.

On the far side of our bed

lies her wooden head-rest.   HITOMARO

It pierces my heel

As I walk in the bedroom:

My late wife's comb.   BUSON

Appreciation of nature, seasonal change, the transience of life, feelings of love and loss: these are some of the great themes common to Japanese poetry throughout its long history. But while the continuity is extraordinary, there is major variation: the work of the four poets in the present collection is diverse and unique.

From medieval poetry to haiku

The classical poems quoted so far come from a type of verse known as *waka*, a word meaning "Japanese poem or song". This term probably came into use in the 9th century, to minimize confusion with the Chinese poetry being read and written by educated Japanese people at a time during the T'ang dynasty when Chinese arts threatened to become overly influential in Japan. It was during this period that Japanese imperial diplomatic and economic ties with China were broken, and consequently Japanese writers were encouraged to pursue more local traditions and genres. Japanese people had been composing *waka* for ceremonial occasions long before the advent of a literary culture, and even when writing become an established means of discourse, the recitation of *waka* remained a public art and means of private communication.

Waka were of two main types: a long form (*choka*) and a short form, later to become known as *tanka*. This shorter variety became Japan's most popular poetic vehicle, and haiku developed from it. Strict rules governed the composition of *tanka*, which consisted of five phrases, each comprising 31 syllables in the following pattern: 5–7–5–7–7. In Japanese script these phrases are set out as vertically aligned characters; English translation renders them conventionally, as lines of poetry.

Most, but not all, *waka* or *tanka* were the work of the educated élite. Calligraphy, musical skill, knowledge of classical poems and the ability to compose original *tanka* were valued aristocratic accomplishments. The voices of the wider population were, nonetheless, never entirely silent. The great national poetry anthologies, the *Man'yoshu* and *Kokinshu* — whose "thousands of leaves" represent the oldest poetic tradition in Japan — contain the songs and poems of common people, priests and soldiers as well as compositions by the nobility. The older of the two collections, the *Man'yoshu*, includes more than 4,000 poems, including pieces from as early as the 5th century. Of special interest to the development of haiku is the division of poems in the *Kokinshu*, compiled around 920CE. Poems are organized according to theme, divided into sections devoted to love and the four seasons. This ordering of topics became prescriptive, and for many centuries determined the subjects that were deemed acceptable for study by the professional poets who made a living giving instruction in haiku writing: the haiku masters.

The development of haiku

As well as governing syllable length and subject matter, classical poetic conventions dictated the language of *tanka*. But reaction against the aristocratic classical *tanka* form set in during the 16th and 17th centuries, when poets began to introduce unorthodox, inelegant language into collectively written linked verses (*renga*). This new "low" language drew on ordinary speech, Chinese, street talk, slang, Buddhist terminology and even obscenities. Sometimes this new poetry derived its character from a single non-classical word. More radical verses mockingly turned convention on its head: a poem by the 16th-century poet Sokan represented the goddess of spring not in a seasonal mist, as convention dictated, but urinating. The tendency toward comic and inelegant subject matter — sex, money, domestic life and other commonplace experiences — was known as *haikai*. The great haiku poets, such as those in this anthology, would develop the restless spirit of *haikai* into a high art.

However, the distinction between classical poetry and *haikai* verse was not absolute. The poet Teitoku, leader of an

early 17th-century *haikai* school, insisted on combining a single *haikai* word into verses that expressed knowledge of the classics. And when the most revered haiku poet Bashō studied with *haikai* master Kigin, he was instructed to immerse himself in classics such as *The Tale of Genji*. Only in this way, Kigin instructed, would he learn to use the spirit of *haikai* in a balanced way. A still more radical approach evolved with the so-called Danrin school based in Osaka in the 1670s. Here, the teacher Soin encouraged students to write spontaneously, break rules by including excess syllables, and write verses linked together by improvisation.

With the 17th century came a growth in urban prosperity, allowing people of the merchant class the leisure to indulge in writing *renga*. Small groups of (usually) men would gather around an experienced poet and collectively write poems whose separate verses were linked by subject, word association, imagery, mood or emotion. A typical *renga* session might last hours, poets taking turns to contribute to a collectively written sequence. Some of the results were a hundred verses long. However, Bashō, who participated in many *renga* gatherings, favoured a 36-poem sequence (*kasen*), which he frequently initiated in the non-classical *haikai* idiom.

In form, the separate stanzas in *renga* were 31-syllable *tankas*, the first and second parts of which comprised 17 and 14 syllables. The opening 17-syllable stanza was generally composed by the master poet, and the name given to this first, important verse was *hokku* (closely related to *haikai*). The term *haiku*, which denotes a free-standing autonomous *hokku* poem, was the invention of the late 19th-century poet Shiki. Here is the beginning of a *renga* jointly composed by Bashō and his disciples. Unusually, the opening *hokku* is by a follower (here, Kyorai). Bashō himself comes in at verse two, capping the first offering by repeating the opening *hokku* and extending it with two 14-syllable phrases:

Even the hawk's feathers

have been smoothed by a passing shower

of early winter rain.   KYORAI

Even the hawk's feathers

have been smoothed by a passing shower

of early winter rain.

   Ruffled by a gust of wind

   dead leaves come to rest again.   BASHŌ

The resulting sequence, with its shifting but internally connected images, moods and improvised poetic associations, is 36 verses long. But however long the *renga* sequence, the opening *hokku* remained the verse of importance, and the status accorded it led to the *hokku*'s recognition as a free-standing, autonomous poem.

The rules of haiku

While some haiku poets claimed a degree of personal freedom, most obeyed decreed compositional rules. First, the haiku consisted of 17 syllables, made up of three phrases of five, seven and five syllables. Within this format, the haiku was generally divided also into two parts standing in contrast or reversal to each other. A poem might start with a traditional image such as cherry blossom, full moon or dew, then re-focus to a "lower", perhaps clashing, image. This poem by Issa expresses an almost brutally comic contrast:

Look at that warbler –

he's wiping his muddy feet

all over the plum blossom.   ISSA

Emphasizing the shift in tone, a "cutting word" (*kireji*)
usually sits at the end of one of the phrases. The cutting word
was often a semantically meaningless sentence-ending
particle such as *kana, ka, ya, keri* or *ran*. Such word sounds did
not themselves contribute meaning but acted both to divide
the poem into two rhythmic halves and to set up a contrast
between the two poem's parts.

A seasonal word (*kigo*) was another prescriptive
component of haiku. Early classical literature contained a
huge vocabulary of words that implied not only a season
but an emotion appropriate to it. Spring, with its mood of
optimism, was implied by cherry blossom and certain birds.
The bright but often fatiguing summer was often suggested
by flower and tree words. Autumn melancholy was expressed
by "lonely" images, such as a full moon, wind and dying leaves.
Cold words, like "snow", alluded to the hard experience of
winter. Poets writing in the spirit of *haikai* added less refined
seasonal words: dandelion, garlic, horseradish and mating
cats all connoted spring, for example.

Other rules underpinned the subtler aspects of haiku. If
classical correctness could be "lowered" to let in descriptions
of ordinary life, it was, said Bashō, important to "correct" the
ordinary, imbuing it with poetic exaltation (*fuga*). In turn,
fuga had to be used to express important ideas: the spiritual
wealth within modest, simple things (*wabi*); beauty, mystery
and elegance (*yugen*), as expressed in the first example by
Bashō, below; and melancholy sadness and tranquillity (*sabi*
and *shiori*), as demonstrated in this second Bashō verse:

Stillness and solitude –

sinking into stones,

the trill of the cicadas.   BASHŌ

On a withered branch

a crow has settled.

Nightfall in autumn.   BASHŌ

The spirit of *haikai* could also be expressed in "poetic
madness" (*fukyo*), well exemplified in one of Bashō's poems
from 1684, and in verse of sometimes shocking comic
"lightness" (*karumi*), as expressed in the second verse below,
from 1690:

Let me show you,

you market people,

this hat filled with snow.   BASHŌ

A bush warbler

leaves its droppings on the rice cake

at the edge of the veranda.   BASHŌ

Both poems express a love of beauty that derives from the
Shinto religion's reverence for landscape and a Buddhist
sense of transience: the vision transmitted by the poets in
this anthology naturally focuses on fleeting impressions of
passing, momentary experience. There is joy in these sharp,
precise perceptions that come alive through their images;
however, there is also an acceptance — sometimes sad —

of life's impermanence. Some of Bashō's poems may be read as demonstrations of genuine Buddhist enlightenment. The truth — the enactment of both the phenomenon, what is, and its passing — is expressed perhaps most vividly in the following celebrated haiku. A creature living unconsciously, according to its nature, is shown in the context of the man-made artifice of an old garden pond, highlighting the simple, bare and eternally ordinary "is-ness" of all existence in the present moment:

Old pond.

A frog jumps in.

The sound of water.   BASHŌ

In many great haiku, seasons and images are suffused with a philosophical mood that introduces a contrast, tension or incongruity into a holistic vision of existence. Haiku, as Bashō said to his Zen teacher, are a description of what is happening at a particular "haiku moment". By presenting imagery that flashes quickly and vividly on the mind's eye, each poem recreates a unique, dramatic scene that expresses emotion and a philosophical awe in the face of some aspect of the natural or social world. Bashō also emphasized sincerity and seriousness (*makoto*): the "poetic truth" of words, which points to a higher reality that can be arrived at through contemplation. By engaging with the great haiku we, as readers, come to an understanding of the poet's thought and vision. To communicate this was the poet's purpose.

The poets in this anthology

The four poets represented here are the most celebrated and best-loved in the Japanese tradition. Though very different poets, each of these haiku masters presents us not only with work of outstanding longevity, but with an example of an artist struggling successfully with difficult and often tragic circumstances. The sublime work of Bashō (c.1644–94) towers above almost everything else. Buson (1716–83), whose genius was expressed in painting as well as poetry, was his more than worthy successor. The deeply humane poet Issa (1762–1826) is perhaps simply the most loved haiku poet, while the poetry of the heroic and tormented Shiki (1867–1902) holds an unassailable place in modern haiku history. Shiki is also remembered as the literary theorist who converted the traditional terms *haikai* and *hokku* into the new word *haiku*, a term suggesting an independent, free-standing, 17-syllable *hokku*-like poem.

Matsuo Bashō (c.1644–94)

Bashō was born into a family of modest circumstances in the city of Ueno, about 30 miles southeast of Kyoto. The poet's father was a minor samurai – one of the warrior caste in the employment of a feudal aristocrat. At the age of nine Bashō was apprenticed to a young samurai who shared with the boy a taste for literature; together they took instruction in poetry-writing. The death of his master in 1666 not only deprived Bashō of an intense friendship, but of a partner for composing linked verse. The young Bashō removed to Kyoto, where he probably practised calligraphy and studied Japanese and Chinese classics. Throughout this time, we must assume that Bashō continued to write linked verse in company, because in search of instruction and an audience he travelled to Edo (modern Tokyo), where he began to consolidate his poetic reputation. It was here that the young Bashō met the poet Soin (1605–82), whose witty and unconventional *haikai* style made a deep impression and prompted Bashō's interest in *renga* of the "lower order" – concerning the ordinary rather than the ideal world. He wrote, "Instead of writing about 'green willows in spring rain', *haikai* (or *renga*) must focus on everyday images, 'such as a crow picking snails out of a rice field.'" Exemplifying this interest in down-to-earth topics, Bashō published witty verses like this:

A tom cat squeezes through

a gap in the hearth

to meet his mistress.   BASHŌ

By the time Bashō had appeared in and edited a number of poetry anthologies — the 17th century saw advances in printing that brought poetry to a considerable audience — the poet had acquired a circle of demanding disciples and felt the need for space and solitude. He moved, in 1680, into a modest hut by a river on the outskirts of Edo, where an admirer presented him with the plantain tree (*bashō*) that would lend its name to a poet who had experimented with a number of pseudonyms. Bashō identified with his non-fruiting banana tree. "I love its uselessness," he wrote. "I sit beneath it and experience the wind and rain that blow against us." Life and poetry-writing were, in other words, simply aspects of nature. To sit with his tree was to participate in the natural world, and the poetry that emerged from this contemplative inactivity fused with phenomena that grew and blew.

The solitary, meditative life that Bashō described beneath his tree harmonized well with the poet's growing interest in Zen Buddhism – the Mahayana Buddhist sect whose practice, imported from T'ang China, was based almost entrely on meditation rather than ritual. The Buddha himself had become enlightened sitting beneath a tree, and the plantain, with its absence of heartwood, was an established Buddhist symbol of impermanence and emptiness. It was during his two-year residence in the plantain tree hut (before it was destroyed by fire in 1682) that Bashō began to study meditation with a local Zen priest by the name of Buccho.

The destruction of his hut proved a turning point in Bashō's career. While the poet's friends built him a new house in the same familiar district, in the summer of 1684 Bashō began the first of the journeys he would describe, unforgettably, in a series of five travel diaries over the next decade. The opening of the first diary, *Records of a Weather-beaten Skeleton*, famously expresses the spiritual fervour of the poet's first setting-out:

"Following the example of the ancient priest who travelled thousands of miles never thinking of his provisions and achieving ecstasy in the pure moon light, I left my little hut on the river as the autumn wind moaned around it."

This journal is unique in Japanese literature and yet develops an existing tradition. As Bashō points out, he is following the example of an ancient priest (probably a reference to a 12th-century Chinese pilgrim). Indeed, as if to emphasize the spiritual nature of his journey, Bashō describes himself in this first journal as a layman with the shaved head of a priest. "I am indeed dressed like a priest," he wrote, "but priest I am not." Examples of travel diaries by other lay people existed in old Japan, the most famous by Lady Sarashina, an 11th-century writer whose prose is punctuated by short, expressive poems. Bashō no doubt had such antecedents in mind when he wrote his travel diaries in the form of prose-and-poetry compositions. This literary genre (*haibun*) allowed Bashō to compose some of his most complex and multi-dimensional writing. On the surface, the diaries have the character of a simple travel narrative – "Readers will find in my diary a random collection of what I have seen on the road," wrote the famous poet somewhat deceptively! On another level, the narrative works as allegory. As Bashō writes at the beginning of an account of his second journey, *Records of a Travel-worn Satchel*, a "wind-swept spirit" in him was "torn and swept away by the slightest breath of wind". His journals, he says, are a record of a spiritual pilgrimage, and the haiku contained in them capture the most profound moments of meditation in the course of a pilgrimage that represents life's journey itself.

The same journal contains another of Bashō's celebrated but enigmatic comments: "All who have achieved excellence in art possess one thing in common: that is, a mind to be one with nature, throughout the seasons." Behind nature's exterior, he states, lie unfathomable meanings that only the poetic imagination can express. "Whatever such a mind sees," Bashō continues, "is a flower, and whatever such a mind dreams of is the moon …" Many of the poet's most celebrated haiku communicate this mysterious symbolic suggestiveness and richness of inner experience.

The journey of 1684 was the first of three long, and many shorter, trips that Bashō would take before his death ten years later. He describes the most demanding trip in *Narrow Road to the Deep North*, a record of 18 months'

travel on foot, between 1689 and 1691. In this classic of exquisite prose and hauntingly evocative poetry, Bashō created the perfect balance between narrative and haiku, the verses embedded within the story. Bashō wrote one haiku at the site of a disastrous battle of the 12th century. From the surface ruins of the battle site, the poet senses the continuing reverberations of deep Japanese history, and comments philosophically on the brevity of life, the emptiness of ambition and the doctrine of impermanence. With a clarity of eye and profundity of imagination, Bashō achieves, within the demands of the 17-syllable haiku, a complex and visionary epic grandeur:

Summer grass.

All that remains

of warriors' dreams.   BASHŌ

Strenuous travelling took its toll. When Bashō embarked, at the age of 50, on his final journey of 1694, his health gave way and he died in the vicinity of Osaka in October of that year. Although far from home, Bashō did not die alone. It was a mark of his achievement that his work was known throughout Japan for much of his life, and that even on journeys he was catered for by strangers in remote places. Bashō's personal life alternated between the solitude of his *bashō* hut and the overwhelming admiration of others. Each extreme was important to his poetry and helped to deepen his vision. As a single man who lived only by his writing, Bashō needed society for its valuable friendship and support. But it was solitude that perhaps led the poet toward insight not available to more gregarious individuals. He often sought out contemplative retreats, such as the

House of the Fallen Persimmons near Kyoto, whose silence, as he wrote, provided an "ideal place for meditation". In the year before his death, Bashō wrote: "When people visit, there is futile talk. When I go out, I feel I'm interfering in the lives of others. I must now emulate the Chinese sages who hid themselves away. Friendlessness will be my companion." Part recluse, part social being, Bashō's hard-won lay Zen practice helped him to achieve balance. "It is important," wrote Bashō, "to keep the mind focused on true [Buddhist] understanding, and then return to the daily world and find truth and beauty there." This vision of poetic truth was dramatically exemplified on a journey with Buccho, his Zen mentor. The priest claimed that poetry was distracting Bashō from his pursuit of enlightenment. Bashō responded by explaining that haiku simply described what happened during one moment of time in a particular place. He then spontaneously composed a verse that Buccho, on hearing, was convinced both exemplified and expressed profound Buddhist insight:

At the road side,

a rose mallow.

My horse has eaten it!   BASHŌ

Yosa Buson (1716–83)

The quality and intensity of haiku writing declined for at least 40 years following Bashō's death, until Buson and a circle of his disciples stimulated a revival of the tradition. Buson's work was in many ways quite different from Bashō's, but because he set out to revive the earlier master's poetic spirit, Buson may be thought of as Bashō's main descendant. Buson himself made this plain when he

declared, "I shall seek only for the elegance, simplicity and sensitivity of old master Bashō and restore *haikai* to what it was in ancient days." Nevertheless, Buson was determined to create an independent style. He proclaimed, "I just move in my own way and enjoy the different atmospheres of yesterday and today."

Buson was forced to contend with an issue relating to the work of Bashō's last years, when he experimented with a new "lightness". Many haiku writers of the succeeding generation followed the same path — with frivolous and empty results. In the mid-18th century, *senryu* poems came into fashion. Structurally identical to haiku, the *senryu* was generally comic, semi-narrative and satirical. This 18th-century trend coincided with growing prosperity and a rise in literacy made possible by advances in printing techniques. And so where haiku had previously been a semi-aristocratic and professional art, amateurs of the growing middle classes now had leisure to dabble, often exploited by poorly qualified "masters". The *haikai* idiom of Bashō's time fell into a conventionalized vulgarism and banality.

Little is known of Buson's social background (he came from a farming district near Osaka), but judging from the energy with which he cultivated a career, we might assume that he did not inherit wealth. What Buson did strive to inherit was the continuity of Bashō's poetic lineage. With this in mind, he travelled to Edo, where as a young man of about 20 he studied with the haiku master Hajin, who had worked with one of Bashō's major associates, the poet Kikaku. Buson remained in Edo until Hajin's death in 1742. In keeping with the seriousness of his ambition, he then tried, unsuccessfully, to establish himself as a poet and painter in Kyoto. Failure lead to a retreat to work in provincial obscurity for more than ten years. During this time of study, Buson developed not just his writing, but his skill in *haiga* – brush painting and haiku combined in one composition. Despite the remote areas in which Buson worked, the artist was able to build a clientele for landscape painting, a genre always popular with the moneyed classes. By 1769 he had established himself as one of Japan's foremost painters, and he returned to Kyoto, where he worked for the rest of his life.

However, commercial success as a painter did not distract Buson from his high artistic ideals. In many ways, Buson, the late 18th-century city dweller, identified himself with classical values derived from ancient China. And so, in addition to his devotion to Bashō, Buson proclaimed a commitment to the path of the amateur (*bunjin*): a career modelled on Chinese "literati" (*wenren*) who, in the Chinese medieval period, practised poetry, painting and calligraphy as a unified art form. If China provided the model, local pressures pushed Buson in the direction of the quiet life of a *bunjin*. In the late 18th century, Japan suffered a terrible onslaught of earthquakes, famine, epidemics and, not least, the maladministration of a corrupt imperial court. Buson's response was to retire from public life and devote himself to his art. In the early years of the 1770s he took on leadership of the so-called Yahantei school of writers — these included Tan Taigi, Chora and Kyotai — who aimed to match the work of Bashō by combining references to contemporary life with a classically elegant style.

The path of the *bunjin* constituted a way of life with both aesthetic and spiritual value. Many of Buson's model Chinese literati were scholars who had retreated from society in pursuit of Taoist or Buddhist contemplative ideals. These ideals, in turn, became the inspiration for their painting and calligraphy – the aim being, through quick and economical brushwork, to express the latent energies of the natural world rather than its literal appearance. But while he studied Chinese masters of poetry, painting and Taoist philosophy, Buson was also well grounded in a more recent Japanese tradition. His spare and allusive painting style was a visual equivalent to the type of haiku Bashō had perfected. Buson's work as poet and painter expresses in equal measure an interest in visual detail, colour, form, imagistic representation and a magical atmosphere of solitude and contemplation.

Though "retired", Buson required social relations with like-minded artists and connoisseurs. As with Bashō before him, the poet worked within a culture which stressed that individual haiku were a constituent part of linked verse. In his earlier years, Buson's creative social life required the discipline of being a student. Later, the disciple took on teaching responsibilities. Paradoxically, Buson learned from his teacher Hajin the necessity of independence. "In the art of *haikai*," Buson recalled his teacher saying, "one should not necessarily follow the diction of one's teacher. A poem should be written suddenly, without consideration of before or after, changing and developing with the moment."

Alluding to Zen Buddhist experience, Buson proclaimed that he had, at the age of 22, achieved "sudden enlightenment under the [haiku] Master's stick, and learned something of what freedom of expression in *haikai* means." The discipline of working within a tradition while pursuing personal independence resembles the process Zen students follow. In one of Buson's most celebrated statements on haiku writing, he declared, very much in the paradoxical manner of a Zen master, "There are no gateways to *haikai*. There is only the *haikai* gateway itself. Great artists do not set up a gateway or school." Most important, suggested Buson, is to be true to your own nature: genuine haiku arise from the personal, inner life. His words sound uncannily modern: "Think for yourself about what you have inside yourself. There is no other way." But then he points out a paradox: in order to arrive at a personal style, the poet must choose appropriate friends to communicate with. Speaking as the leader of a Kyoto haiku circle, Buson may be describing himself and his experienced colleagues. But he also refers to something more classical and mysterious:

"Day after day you should get away from distracting cities and go to meet these poets. Walk in the forest and the mountains. This way you acquire *haikai* naturally. And then one day you will meet those poets, and you will close your eyes and seek words. When a *haikai* comes, you will open your eyes. The poets will have gone. ... You're alone and in ecstasy. There will be the scent of flowers on the wind. Moonlight on the water. This is the world of *haikai*."

To appreciate Buson's poetry, and his teaching ("Be separate from the ordinary. But still use the ordinary"), compare a haiku he wrote about a willow tree with a verse on the same tree by Bashō from 1689, and the original verse describing the willow by their literary ancestor, the 12th-century poet Saigyo:

By the roadside,

by a clear stream

in the shade of a willow

I paused – I thought

for just a moment.   SAIGYO

A whole field they sowed.

Only then did I get up

from Saigyo's willow.   BASHŌ

Fallen leaves around the willow.

The stream dried up.

A scattering of stones.   BUSON

While Saigyo and Bashō write spring poems, Buson's "fallen
leaves" suggest an autumn scene. And where Bashō composes
a contemplative evocation of Saigyo's 12th century and
his own more recent moments under the willow, Buson
presents a beautiful, if melancholy, visual scene. Time is
suggested by the immediacy of autumn, which draws
together tree, stream-bed and stones. The words are almost
as vivid as if the poet had painted the scene. The best of
Buson's poems are marked by a similar imagistic vitality.
One of his most celebrated shows a peony in close-up
(almost cinematic) slow-motion. Another poem focuses on
an axe-head at the moment it contacts a tree-trunk. By
closing in on both axe and tree, the poem enacts the
sensation of resistance from living wood that reveals life in
the trunk, the poet's physical experience and his awareness
of its significance:

Peony petals fall,

piling one on another,

first two, then three.   BUSON

The bite of my axe.

Sudden revelation –

there's life in this tree!   BUSON

Mystery informs Buson's haiku. They can be visually bright,
yet remain thematically remote. In his famous kite poem
(below), kite and sky are superimposed visually, in a clear
image, but large, enigmatic questions hang unanswered.
Does this kite (a spring-season word) represent his
childhood? And how does the poet imagine the space to
have changed since that time? The poet was also fascinated
by the mystery of Japanese and Chinese folklore about
animals and spirits. Buson specialized in compressing the
action of entire narratives, as in the "short story" (also
quoted below) that opens and closes within 17 syllables:

A paper kite flies

just where it was

in yesterday's sky.   BUSON

They escaped with their lives,

managed to get married.

They can, at last, change their clothes.   BUSON

On his deathbed, Buson composed poems that bear direct
comparison with the haiku Bashō wrote in his final hours.
Both writers composed several haiku that remain sublime in
their sadness and acceptance. Bashō's death poem suggests
the end of a life's journey filled with equal parts imaginative
dreaming and melancholy insight. The imagery of his haiku

is simultaneously vague and grand, the emotion imbued with an apprehension of mortality. Buson's death poem has an equally powerful suggestion of finality. His last night is certainly dark. However, it is illuminated with a lovely, optimistic image of plum blossom that grows ever more distinct as dawn breaks and the poet anticipates a morning that he may not see. He accepts this quietly, and leaves the world with a farewell that has endured:

Laid waste on this journey.

My dreams wander scattered

through desolate fields.   BASHŌ

White plum blossoms.

Night turns to dawn –

The time has come.   BUSON

Kobayashi Issa (1762–1826)

If Bashō is acknowledged as the supreme master of haiku, Issa is one of the great originals of world poetry and undoubtedly the best loved of the major Japanese poets. This is not to suggest that Issa does not command the respect due to a great poet. Rather, it is that his warm, childlike and sometimes zany personality elicits affection and sympathetic amusement at the constantly surprising beauty of his poems. Where Bashō is austere and exalted and Buson coolly precise, Issa is excitable, impulsive and explosively engaged with the world. Whether he laughs, suffers or cries out in wonder, he draws us companionably to his side. "Issa opens his soul to us," wrote a Japanese commentator. "For this reason we love him."

From early childhood, Yataro Kobayashi's was a life of almost unrelieved tragedy ("Issa" was a pen name). His mother died while he was a baby, the young poet was exploited and deprived of his property rights by an almost storybook stepmother, and in adulthood his first two wives died. Compounding these tragedies, Issa lost all his children as infants and died heart-broken when the family house that he had finally retrieved from his stepmother burned to the ground. Fortunately, Issa had the opportunity to leave home at the age of 14, and found some fulfilment in Edo, where, in 1787, he apprenticed himself to a haiku master who recognized his talent. Abandoning the capital after his master's death, Issa was ordained as a Buddhist priest of the Shin (Pure Land) sect and spent the next decade as a homeless wanderer. In taking to the road, Issa followed the tradition of the Buddhist pilgrim poet exemplified by Bashō a century earlier. But while Bashō's travelling represented time-limited journeys into meditative solitude, Issa's life of wandering was both an expression of chronic homelessness and an opportunity to connect with the world. This connection with the world was all-embracing: the wandering poet loved, above all, to play with children he met in the villages he passed through and to commune with any other, non-human, beings he encountered. This is reflected in his poetry. For while Issa could, at will, deploy traditional images of cherry blossom and butterflies, his playful and inclusive imagination also delighted in living things — ants, flies, snails, poisonous mushrooms, mosquitoes — that most people found repellent. In choosing such ostentatiously "low" topics for his poetry, Issa was not just expressing an idiosyncratic compassion, he was subtly and self-consciously placing himself within the haiku tradition. Bashō had shown that ordinary, down-to-earth subject matter could be converted into great poetry. And while Issa took such "vulgarity" of content to a new extreme, he, like Bashō, was more than capable of transforming it into glowingly beautiful and often witty haiku:

This mushroom is

deadly. And, of course,

it's also very pretty.   ISSA

Issa's choice of subject emerged from an extraordinary sensitivity to a world that was both difficult and thrillingly beautiful. As a bereaved child, Issa is said to have composed his first poem at the sight of a fledgling sparrow that had fallen from its nest:

Come on: let's play

together, then,

little motherless sparrow!   ISSA

Although unlikely to be true, the story gives an important insight about the poet. Firstly, it shows how Issa's enthusiastic genius gives rise to apparently spontaneous poetry. Secondly, the story reveals how a life-long psychological wound drew the poet to seek consolation in playful friendships with other marginal beings. Thirdly, and no less importantly, the story highlights his compassion for the suffering of other creatures. It is relevant here to remember Issa's identity as a Buddhist. In contrast to Bashō, who was drawn to the austerity of Zen with its emphasis on insight into Buddhist doctrine, Issa's Buddhism proclaimed the brotherhood of beings. And while many of Issa's poems are highly subjective, his compassion leads him to place the other — whatever its nature — at precisely his own level:

Just one man and

one fly in this

enormous guest-room.

ISSA

Issa's love of the humble and ordinary was matched by his self-presentation. He cultivated a dirty and unkempt appearance, and his manners were often unconventional and intentionally rude. The language of Issa's poetry is also sometimes deliberately rough and unpolished. He eschewed literary language and wrote in the vernacular, frequently deploying local dialect and slang in keeping with a poetic vision of a world that was at once exquisite and grubby. His famous lines, "Look at that warbler – wiping his dirty feet on the plum blossom," sum this up very well. Part of the beauty of the world, suggests Issa, lies in its imperfection. Lovely, pure-looking things of the air get mixed in and messed up with grimy stuff from the earth, and it is the poet's task to point this out. Issa's adopted name was another statement about himself and the nature of the world. Bashō took an earthy pseudonym with Buddhist connotations (see pages 22–3). Issa followed suit in 1792, characteristically taking a step further: he chose a name that means "Cup of Tea". Like much of his poetry, this smacks of the profound as well as the absurd. Green tea served in the Japanese tea ceremony is carefully whisked to create a surface froth, and so Issa's playfully adopted name suggests both the transient nature of existence, to which the idea of "foam" alludes, and also a ceremonial quality,

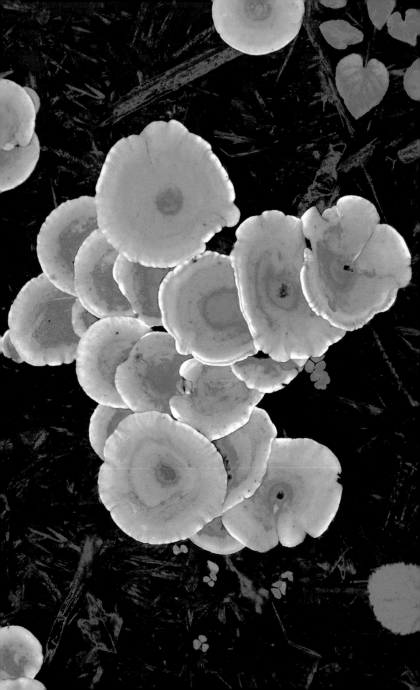

recalling the quiet austerities of the tea ceremony. In his short, fragmentary autobiographical prose-and-verse book, *The Year of My Life*, a semi-fictionalized account of the year 1819, Issa explained further:

"There's a poet who runs east one day and west the next day, like a mad man. He's as helpless as the waves on the shore. His life is as transient as foam that vanishes in a moment. This is why this poet calls himself 'Cup of Tea'."

Two more passages from *The Year of My Life* point to the ambiguity of Issa's self-perception and the nature of his dual identity as poet and priest. The opening of Chapter Four of his autobiography echoes Bashō's travel journals when he writes:

"At long last I made up my mind to travel north this year to gain more experience in writing haiku. As soon as I had slung my beggar's bag around my neck, I noted with surprise that my shadow looked identical to that of Saigyo, the poet-priest [of the 12th century]."

Issa hints here that he is following Bashō's northward journey just as Bashō followed Saigyo and earlier Chinese sages to places of pilgrimage. And while this indicates the seriousness of Issa's undertaking, the next passage is humbling: "However, I was much ashamed when I reflected how different his mind was from mine — his white, pure as snow, mine black as coal …"

In Chapter Two of *The Year of My Life,* Issa narrates the poignant story of the drowning of a small boy. When the boy's body is recovered, some blossom is found in his pocket, which Issa suggests is a gift for his parents. Despite being Buddhist priests used to preaching indifference to life's vicissitudes, they run up to the body and weep bitterly. "Who can blame them," continues Issa. "It is only human that their hearts should be deeply oppressed by their unbreakable attachment to the child." The touching details of this story might apply to the poet himself. For he, too, was a man deeply attached to the world, who freely acknowledged his own suffering. Priest though he was, he dedicated his suffering, and the compassionate Buddhist vision that this opened for him, to the creation of passionately original poetry. Such openness and warmth may explain why Issa remains the most loved of poets.

Masaoka Shiki (1867–1902)

Born in the very last year of the feudalistic Tokugawa era and at the beginning of the modernizing Meiji period, Shiki was the son of a failed samurai. His grandfather was a strict Confucian who emphasized the importance of tradition. If his grandson were to become a Japanese poet, the old man warned him at the opening of an era of increasing influence from the West, he must avoid contamination from European writing that "crawls sideways like a crab". In becoming a deeply knowledgeable scholar and writer of Japanese poetry, Shiki took his grandfather's advice. But like the great haiku writers before him, the poet also drew inspiration from the historical changes that touched him.

Shiki was a delicate youth, and his fragile health made studying difficult. He enrolled at several universities and intermittently, over a number of years, studied literature, philosophy and aesthetics, eventually withdrawing from academic life in 1892, restlessly drawn, as he was, to writing

poetry and particularly, as he later wrote, "bewitched by the goddess of haiku". For the rest of his short life, Shiki devoted himself almost entirely to the rehabilitation of the haiku tradition which, by the 19th century, had declined into mediocrity and conventionality.

Shiki pursued his literary career in three distinct but interconnected ways. As a self-taught scholar, he set about studying the *tanka* and *haikai* canon in order to arrive at an understanding of the spirit of haiku. In the course of this exploration, he embarked on a colossal project to compile a *Classified Collection of Haiku*. To support himself and other poets, and to underpin his role as haiku polemicist, Shiki also became a literary journalist. Between 1892 and his death in 1902 he wrote many important articles, as haiku editor of the newspaper *Nippon* and from 1897 as co-founder of the literary magazine *Hototogisu*. Most importantly, Shiki became a *haijin, or* "haiku person": a dedicated haiku poet.

Shiki's scholarly work and literary journalism took him into fascinating and sometimes contentious territory. In 1893, his notorious controversial essay, *Some Remarks on Bashō*, shocked the public by criticizing a large body of Bashō's work for the vagueness of its "broad outline" and its frequent dependence (in the travel journals) on prose explanation. Shiki recognized Bashō's major work for its grandeur, and lamented the dramatic decline in the *hokku* tradition that followed the master's death. But he attacked the canonization that elevated Bashō the man to saintly status and his poetry to a religious text. Bashō was, according to Shiki, a great poet, but he lacked imagination and wrote – as Bashō himself acknowledged to his Zen teacher – largely about the world around him.

Shiki's negativity toward Bashō is sometimes exaggerated to the detriment of his more significant contribution to literary history: his championing of Yosa Buson. Although Buson's work as a painter continued to be admired in the 19th century, his poetry had become almost entirely neglected. In discussing the difference between Bashō and Buson, Shiki suggested that Bashō's greatness lay in a "negative beauty" characterized by "classical grace, mystery, depth, serenity, simplicity and a subdued elegance". In contrast, Buson's "positive" traits lay, he said, in the "virility, power, charm and liveliness" of his haiku. Most importantly to Shiki, Buson's work had an imaginative power that reached into unknown dimensions – myth or narrative mystery, for instance, as demonstrated in the first example below. The detailed, painterly clarity of Buson's writing in the second example also appealed to Shiki:

Who is this suspicious couple

resting at the tea-house

with the wisteria blossom?   BUSON

An old bagworm cocoon.

Next to this hangs

two plum blossoms.   BUSON

Whatever the truth of Shiki's remarks about the relative value of his two great literary ancestors, his single-handed rehabilitation of Buson's poetry not only helped to establish an enduring Japanese poetic canon, but also emboldened Shiki's own poetic enterprise. By the end of this poet's life, the four-person foundation of the haiku tradition would in the future – and enduringly – consist of Bashō, Buson, Issa and Shiki himself.

One aspect of Shiki's life cannot be overemphasized: chronic ill-health not only tragically curtailed his life, but brought intense physical pain when, in his final years, the poet was bed-ridden and scarcely able to hold a writing brush. Shiki noticed the first symptoms of incurable tuberculosis in 1889, when the poet found himself spitting blood. It was at this point that he adopted the name Shiki, which alluded to the four seasons and also to the Japanese cuckoo (*hototogisu*) which, according to legend, spits blood as it sings. As tubercular infection attacked his spine, the unrelieved pain triggered by the slightest movement did nothing to subdue the energy and idealism of Shiki's poetry and journalism, and much of his greatest work emerged from the experience of pain and isolation.

As early as 1890, Shiki started following, in a modified way, the example set by Bashō when he embarked on relatively limited haiku-writing journeys. But while Bashō often travelled to places with historical and literary associations, Shiki largely disregarded the literary-historical tradition, insisting on a poetry of direct, spontaneous observation that expressed the quality of "as is": the reality of the rural and urban scenes that he routinely witnessed. This method brought together aspects of Bashō and Buson's work: Shiki brought a spontaneous and often highly informal realism into the culture of a rapidly modernizing late 19th-century Japan. The resulting poetry was almost always startlingly fresh – frequently juxtaposing a taste of the present with a background of ancient life, apprehended in the contemporary moment. One of Shiki's best-known poems, alluding to the 8th-century Buddhist temple of Horyuji in the ancient capital city of Nara, evocatively brings together the intensity of taste and touch in the present moment with a sound that, to the Japanese imagination, stretches back through the centuries:

As I bite a persimmon

a bell rings out –

Horyuji.   SHIKI

Painting was a preoccupation, and in the mid-1890s Shiki met the painter Nakamura Fusetsu, whose work he published in *Nippon* and through whom he developed the practice of writing "sketches from life" (*shasei*). Among his sketches are many haiku depicting sports events and popular celebrations:

Everyone's gone home.

The fireworks are over.

How dark it has become!   SHIKI

As Shiki's sickness intensified in the late 1890s, many of his poems reflected his suffering and approaching death. He poignantly described his poetry of this period as being "like drops squeezed from a nearly dried-up brush." The following haiku combine eerie echoes of the old haiku tradition with the weary, down-to-earth realities of his monotonous condition:

An old garden. Under

the moon, she empties

my stone hot-water bottle.   SHIKI

Again and again

I ask how high the

snow outside is piled ...   SHIKI

Shiki's was a short and tragic life, yet his late poems are
comparable to the final verses written by Bashō and Buson
when, as older men, they approached death. All three great
writers faced their end with both gravity and courage.
Shiki's last poems, penned shortly before he died in 1902,
treat death with a similarly stark, matter-of-fact simplicity.
This is the end, these poems imply, but death is ordinary.
A domestic event. It is in the nature of things. Shiki was
not a religious poet like Bashō and Issa, nor did he attempt
to imbue his work with an overt philosophical message.
It is Shiki's brilliance of language and his heroic literary
idealism that place his work securely at the centre
of the tradition that his great predecessors had
established for him to extend.

The Haiku

Bashō (c.1644–94)

Wind in autumn –

a door slides open

and a sharp cry comes through.

Into my gate of brushwood sticks

the wind sweeps

tea leaves.

"Little pine" is a gentle name,

and the wind blows softly

through the pampas grass and clover.

Already I can see

my own wind-bleached bones.

A cold wind cuts me.

Poets moved by the monkey's cry:

what would you feel for this abandoned child

in the cold wind this autumn?

Darkening sea.

The cry of wild duck

faintly white.

Azaleas in a wooden pail.

A woman tears up dried fish

in their shade.

Violets, as I walk

this mountain road,

draw me to them somehow.

Just butterflies

and sunlight

in the whole empty meadow.

First light snowfall.

But heavy enough

to bend daffodil leaves.

The broom forgets

about the snow

as it sweeps the garden.

Winter chrysanthemums

covered with rice bran

scattered from the mortar.

The language of these samurai

tastes pungent

as radish.

Plum blossom scent

as the sun comes up

on a path through the mountains.

It should have

stayed green,

this bright red pepper!

The black eyes of white fish

open

in the net of dharma*.

Moon flowers in the garden –

I poke my drunk face

out of the window.

*ultimate truth

Again waiting for you at night.

And the cold wind

turns to rain.

The great Buddha does nothing.

He doesn't even blink

at falling hailstones.

A moonlit night,

and a flock of wild geese

fly low across the railway line.

Old pond.

Upside down

the shell of a cicada floats there.

Surrounded by islands,

each one with its pine trees

and the cool sound of wind.

A fierce autumn wind,

and a snake falls off

a high stone wall.

Further reading

Bashō, M., translated by Yuasa, N. *The Narrow Road to the Deep North and other Travel Sketches*, Penguin, London 1966

Beichman, J. *Masaoka Shiki*, Cheng & Tsui, Kodansha 2002

Blyth, R.H. *Haiku*, Hokuseido Press, Tokyo 1949–52

Bownas, G. and Thwaite, A. *The Penguin Book of Japanese Verse*, Penguin, London 1964

Hass, R. *The Essential Haiku*, Ecco Press, New York 1994

Henderson, H.G. *An Introduction to Haiku*, Doubleday, New York 1958

Issa, K., translated by Yuasa, N. *A Year in My Life*, University of California Press, Berkeley 1972

Keene, D. *Anthology of Japanese Literature from the Earliest Era to the Mid-nineteenth Century*, Grove Press, New York 1955

Keene, D. *World Within Walls*, Columbia University Press, New York 1999

Miner, E. *Japanese Linked Poetry*, Princeton University Press, Princeton 1979

Miner, E. *The Monkey's Straw Raincoat*, Princeton University Press, Princeton 1981

Sato, H. and Watson, B. *From the Country of Eight Islands*, University of Washington Press, Washington 1981

Shiki, M., translated by Watson, B. *Selected Poems*, Columbia University Press, New York 1997

Shirane, H. *Traces of Dreams: The Poetry of Bashō*, Stanford University Press, Palo Alto 1998

Ueda, M. *Bashō and his Interpreters*, Stanford University Press, Palo Alto 1991

Ueda, M. *Matsuo Bashō*, Twayne Publishers, New York 1970

Index

The poets

Matsuo Bashō (c.1644–94): Considered the greatest of the haiku poets
Nozawa Bonchō (died 1714): Physician who became an important disciple of Bashō
Yosa Buson (1715–83): Great haiku poet and painter
Chinseki: Poet and associate of Bashō
Etsujin (1656-1739)
Fubakū: Associate of Bashō
Fumikuni: Associate of Bashō; co-wrote *The Monkey's Straw Raincoat*
Kakinomoto no Hitomaro (active c.700): Major classical poet of the *Man'yoshu*
   anthology
Kobayashi Issa (1762–1826): Great haiku poet and Shin Buddhist priest
Takarai Kikaku (1661-1707): Bashō's foremost disciple
Ono no Komachi (mid-9th century): A famous beauty and classical poet
Takechi no Kurohito (active 8th century): Author of famous *tanka* and *waka* that
   evoke his travels
Mukai Kyorai (1651–1704): One of Bashō's major disciples
Ranran: Disciple of Bashō
Saigyo (1118–90): Major travelling priest poet
Masaoka Shiki (1867–1902): Major haiku poet and literary historian
Prince Shiki (668–716): Son of emperor Tenji and author of six *waka* in *Man'yoshu*
Murasaki Shikibu (c.973 – c.1020): author of *The Tale of Genji* and many *waka*
Shohaku (1649-1722)
Sogi (1421–1501): Major poet of linked verses
Sora (1648-1710): Poet who accompanied Bashō on the journey north
Yoshinaga Tangan: Associate of Bashō

About the author/photographer

Tom Lowenstein is a poet, anthropologist and cultural historian. His previous
books include *Buddhist Inspirations* and *Haiku Inspirations* (both DBP) and several
collections of poetry, including, most recently, *Ancestors and Species*.

John Cleare is an internationally renowned photographer specializing in mountains
and landscapes. His photographs illustrate an edition of the *Tao Te Ching* (Watkins
publishing) and *Tales from the Tao* (DBP).

Children!

Look, the bindweed is in flower.

I'll peel us a melon.

Autumn wind.

The mulberry branch

lies sadly broken.

Between the stones

in the mason's yard

chrysanthemums are flowering.

One hydrangea bush and a tangled thicket

make up the small garden

for this cottage.

Asleep at noon

the heron's body

nobly poised.

On the bare earth

in the morning dew,

cool, mud-splashed melons.

Drooping

in this upside-down world,

a bamboo in the snow.

———

Waves on blue sea,

the smell of *sake*.

A harvest moon rises.

Rainy season

and the crane's legs

have grown shorter.

Autumn deepens.

What is my neighbour doing,

I wonder?

Why do I feel so old

this autumn?

A bird flies through the clouds.

The beginning of all art:

a rice planting song

in a remote district.

Autumn nightfall

and the long road

empty.

Laid waste on this journey.

My dreams wander scattered

through desolate fields.

On a withered branch

a crow has settled.

Nightfall in autumn.

How many old memories

they bring to mind –

the cherry blossoms.

I dozed on my horse –

half-dreaming, the moon distant,

breakfast tea steaming.

Autumn wind. My plantain tree.

Night rain patters

into a basin.

Stillness and solitude –

sinking into stones,

the trill of the cicadas.

Out over the fields,

attached to nothing,

a skylark sings.

Don't eat that horsefly

at play in the blossoms,

my friend sparrow.

Wake up, butterfly!

Come on – wake up!

I want friendship.

Softly fluttering,

yellow roses drop.

The waterfall roaring.

A solitary hawk,

how happy I was to find it

at Irako Point.

Delightful and yet

presently how saddening,

the boats of the cormorant fishers.

A flash of lightning

and then darkness.

The night cry of a heron.

In my humble view

hell must be

an autumn evening.

Quietly in the night,

a worm in moonlight

burrows through a chestnut.

Old pond.

A frog jumps in.

The sound of water.

As the bell's notes fade

the scent of cherry lingers.

Evening twilight.

Over the dead grass

heat waves shimmer

just an inch or two.

Daffodils

and a white paper screen

reflect each other's colour.

Quietly drinking tea,

a Buddhist monk.

Chrysanthemum blossoms.

Scattered islands

in thousands of pieces:

the sea in summer.

Come and walk

to view the snow –

till I slip and fall over!

A sad fate for us all:

we feed bamboo shoots

at the inescapable conclusion!

Sparrows in a rape field

look as though

they're out to view blossom.

Following the sun

the hollyhocks turn

in summer rainfall.

A dragonfly

struggles to grip

a grass blade.

Washed clean, spring onions

gleam white

in the cold weather.

I've lived for so long

that all I can do

is suck these fish bones.

Under the cherry tree,

eating soup, fish and vegetables

with petals scattered on them.

Under a bright moon,

walking all night

around the pool.

Seasonal Interlude

Winter

Time of winter drizzle.

The only light comes

from the charcoal shop window.

BONCHŌ

Out-of-season cherries.

Let's lay out some straw mats

and sit down to eat them.

KIKAKU

This ancient temple

has floor-slats turned green

in the cold mid-winter.

BONCHŌ

In spite of the cold,

winter peonies, naked and leafless,

are in flower.

SHARAI

With useless authority

the great horned owl

sits moon-eyed in daylight.

KAIKYO

Plovers on the beach.

The wolf's tracks

are crossed out and rewritten.

FUMIKUNI

Moving silhouettes of fish

beneath the ice.

Cormorants in torment.

TANGAN

It travels on and on,

the river in one dark line

across the snow fields.

BONCHŌ

Spring

The first butterfly of spring.

This creature without bones

alights on stiff plum blossom.

HANZAN

Alongside the hedge

the white plum blossoms

by the ash tip.

BONCHŌ

The temple bell at twilight

presses on the plum trees

its reverberations.

FUBAKŪ

Between patches of ice

a few scattered flowers

of what seems to be parsley.

KIKAKU

A warbler singing.

Mud catches the teeth of my clogs

beside the rice fields.

BONCHŌ

I envy the tom cat:

how easily he lets go of

love's pain and longing!

ETSUJIN

In the shimmer of spring air

the fox cubs are allowed their play time

as their parents watch them.

BONCHŌ

A butterfly arrived

and spent the whole night sleeping

on the top of a spring onion.

HANZAN

Summer

Thatching the roof

he interweaves

the leaves of the blue iris.

KIKAKU

The lovely broad leaves

of the striped bamboo

with rice dumplings in them.

GANO

Summer rain.

In just one night

my razor has rusted over.

BONCHŌ

As they catch at each other

you can just see children's heads

above the barley.

YUTO

The child cries at her breast.

And the mosquito also bites

the sleeping mother.

RANRAN

The bargeman's wife

sings as she pulls the boat upsteam

past flowering silk trees.

SENNA

With ink-stained lips,

the boy leaves his poem

for the cool outdoors.

SENNA

Autumn

Just like us, the monkey

folds its arms on its chest

in the cold autumn wind.

CHINSEKI

Sleepless all night

in the constant autumn wind

in far-off mountains.

SORA

In the first autumn dew,

the boar's outline on the grass

where he got up from sleep.

KYORAI

A freezing wind

accompanies the lonely moon

in the autumn sky.

BONCHŌ

No rain for days,

and now tonight it's come

and screens the moon off.

SHOHAKU

I thinned out the chrysanthemums,

but the field I left behind

looked no different at all.

KIKAKU

As I leave the house

on an autumn evening,

the wind brings on a rash.

BONCHŌ

Buson (1715–83)

Fallen leaves around the willow.

The stream dried up.

A scattering of stones.

Wading through a stream

in summer, carrying my sandals.

How delightful!

Divorced and lonely,

she walks to the field

to help plant seedlings.

A lightning flash.

Encircled by waves,

the islands of Japan.

Camphor tree roots

that winter rain

has gently moistened.

Peony petals fall,

piling one on another,

first two, then three.

The bite of my axe.

Sudden revelation:

there's life in this tree!

Spring's passing already.

The lute in my hands

seems suddenly heavier.

A paper kite flies

just where it was

in yesterday's sky.

Long, slow spring days,

one following another.

The past recedes so!

Was that a fox

or a prince in disguise

this hazy spring evening?

The plum trees are white.

Who, from the deep past,

stands outside my fence?

The plum trees are in bloom.

The long night brings the dawn.

My time has come at last.

Confidently rising

among vigorous young leaves,

this hill-top castle.

Autumn rains,

and two little houses

by the swollen river.

In the cool of morning

the bell's voice

leaves the bell.

They escaped with their lives,

managed to get married.

They can, at last, change their clothes.

Young squire

throwing off his robes

in the mist, in the moonlight.

Burdened with dark thoughts

I climbed the hill to find

wild roses blooming.

A breeze this evening

and little waves splash

the shins of a blue heron.

A flock of sparrows

in a sudden shower

clinging to dry grasses.

I go out to my garden

to pick a melon.

What a thief I am!

Flowering bindweed

wraps the fence posts of a patch

the town's creeping up on.

At the end of the path

the overpowering scent

of flowers on a thorn bush.

Here is the end –

my path has vanished

into the parsley.

Shaped by the path

the pilgrims' chant grows thinner

on this winter evening.

Who is this suspicious couple

resting at the tea house

with the wisteria blossom?

Deep in the old well

the dark sound of fish

leaping at mosquitoes.

Just enough spring rain

to wet all the seashells

on the shoreline.

A builder tramples the dry leaves

on the roof

above my bedroom.

Long heavy rain

has brought life back

to the dried seaweed on the beach

It stands guard on the flowers

without bow and arrows,

this solitary scarecrow.

A field covered with thorns.

But nightfall brings

lovely insect song!

How fine to see

the pure white fan

of my beloved!

Once beyond the gate

I too am a traveller

in the autumn twilight.

In shimmering heat waves –

I don't know what they're called –

these little white insects.

An old bagworm cocoon.

Next to this hangs

two plum blossoms.

After it has dropped,

the image of a peony

haunts me.

Autumn evening.

With her sleeve

she wipes a mirror.

Here and in the distance,

the sound of rain through

the young leaves falling.

Thinner and thinner grows
the moon,

and then it's gone.

The night is colder.

Against a gold screen,

radiantly splendid,

this flowering peony.

Ant on

white peony.

Contrast brilliant!

Wheat-harvesting time.

The lonely face

of this crazy woman.

Heavy autumn rain.

Muddy river plunges

into blue sea water.

Yellow mustard flowers.

No inshore whales in sight.

Night falls on the ocean.

A quick rattle of hail,

as day breaks,

on the camellia leaves.

Winter. The cold

lingers in this scarf

of light blue material.

Extricating itself from thorns,

a bush warbler

soars high.

So distant from the moon –

the colour and scent

of wisteria blossom.

Issa (1762–1826)

New Year's day –

but my tumbledown hut

looks the same as ever!

A rainy day in spring,

and this thrown-away letter

blows around among the trees.

Alone among the shady bushes

a girl is singing

a rice-planter's song.

Is that crow tilling

the field or just

walking around there?

The cat sleeps. It gets up.

It gives a great yawn.

And off it goes now to make love!

In my home village

I left so long ago

the cherry trees are blooming.

Look at that warbler –

he's wiping his muddy feet

all over the plum blossom.

Little snail,

slowly, slowly,

climbs Mount Fuji.

Midday – and the cheep of

buntings. But the river itself

is completely silent.

Watch that giant firefly!

It's zigzagging all over the place.

Gone now …

Just one man and

one fly in this

enormous guest-room.

Crawling across this high

rope-bridge, I hear from below

a cuckoo calling.

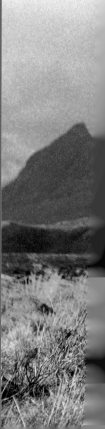

Those distant mountains

reflected in the

eye-jewels of the dragonfly.

All buckled and bent

this three-day-old moon.

An intense coldness.

How beautiful to see

the Milky Way through

a hole in the window.

This mushroom is

deadly. And, of course,

it's also very pretty.

A butterfly in the garden.

The baby crawls. The butterfly flies.

The baby crawls. Off the butterfly flies.

Don't cry, little insects!

Love involves parting.

It even happens among the stars.

Lying on the grass

I pluck fresh herbs

in the sun.

How beautiful the sky is

when a lark

has been singing.

Falling leaves

silently

intensify the cold.

A sparrow is flying

in and out of

the jail house.

Shiki (1867–1902)

From somewhere

at the back of the shoe cupboard

a cricket is singing.

Far away and high

above the trees

fireworks are exploding.

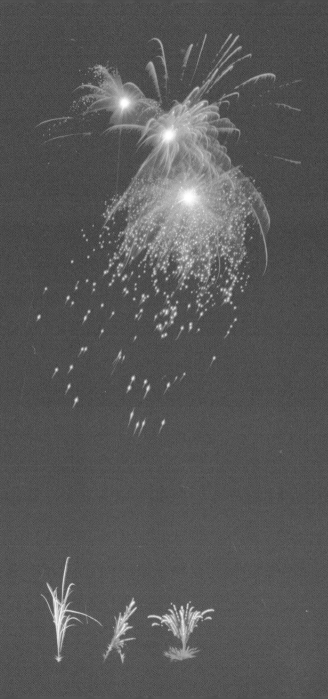

That one rock in the field:

someone's always lying

on it in the summer.

I climb into bed

and *then* take my socks off.

How lazy I'm getting!

Flowering on the hilltop

where a castle once stood:

daikon radishes.

Sunrise.

Through my mosquito net

I see a white sail passing.

Wind in summer:

and all my unlined writing

paper's blowing off my desk.

Wheat harvest in autumn.

Boys walloping a snake

on a country road.

Someone has managed to

light a fire in the builders'

shed this foggy morning.

This year I fell ill when

the peonies were in flower,

and got better with the chrysanthemums.

Meadow in summer.

People playing baseball

somewhere in the distance.

A broken clog-strap

left out in the

winter rice fields.

After I'm dead, tell people

I was a persimmon eater

who also loved haiku.

Still-life sketching.

Aubergines are more

difficult than pumpkins.

These purple grapes –

so dark they're

almost black!

The lamp in the next room

goes out too.

A cold, cold night.

The lonely circle of the moon.

Countless stars

in a dark green sky.

A stream that runs through

the centre of the village,

and the willows growing next to it.

They have chopped down

the willow tree. So

the kingfishers have also vanished.

Plum blossoms falling

on the *koto**.

Evening moonlight.

*Japanese lute

How cool it has become!

I've completely forgotten

that I'd planned to steal some melons.

A flash of lightning.

Between trees in the forest

I caught a glimpse of water.

A river in summer.

There's a bridge here, but

my horse prefers the water.

In crevice after crevice

on the cliff face –

wild azaleas.

Perched on a mud wall,

a crow sits

in the light spring rain.

How lonely I felt

on a cold, cold night

when I killed that spider.

Swat those flies

softly please.

I want to sleep.

I think I'd like to die

eating apples

with a view of peonies.